This journal belongs to

....

Date ....

"*From the garden...at the foot of Mount Gerizim we could often watch the gazelles bounding up the mountainside, leaping from rock to rock with extraordinary grace and agility. Their motion was one of the most beautiful examples of exultant and apparently effortless ease in surmounting obstacles which I have ever seen.*"

How deeply we who love the Lord of Love and desire to follow Him long for the power to surmount all difficulties and tests and conflicts in life in the same exultant and triumphant way.

Hannah Hurnard

Introduction

You are a beloved child of God, precious to Him in every way. As you seek Him, He will guide you along paths you may or may not be sure of, but His presence will be with you in the High Places. God cares about you and knows the desires of your heart. Wherever you are along the way, He is as close as breathing.

Excerpts (italicized throughout) from Hannah Hurnard's beautifully written allegory guide you through the story of Much-Afraid's journey to the High Places. We invite you to use this journal as a companion to her classic book or to document your own journey— to express your thoughts and prayers, write down your fears and your victories, and find strength through God to accomplish all that He has planned for you. Let it be an ongoing record of your walk with the Chief Shepherd.

Be strong in Him. And may the Lord of Love guide your heart always.

He makes my feet like hinds' feet,
and sets me upon my high places.

PSALM 18:33 NASB

Perfect Love Casts Out Fear

This is the story of how Much-Afraid escaped from her Fearing relatives and went with the Shepherd to the High Places where "perfect love casteth out fear."... She was a cripple [and had] a crooked mouth...and was sadly conscious that these [offended] many who knew that she was in the service of the great Shepherd....

She longed to be completely delivered from these shortcomings and to be made beautiful, gracious, and strong as were so many of the Shepherd's other workers, and above all to be made like the Chief Shepherd himself.

As love has its perfect way, it leads us into purity of heart. When we are perpetually bombarded by the rapturous experience of divine love, it is only natural to want to be like the Beloved.

RICHARD FOSTER

O this full and perfect peace,

O this transport all divine—

In a love which cannot cease,

I am His, and He is mine.

GEORGE WADE ROBINSON

There is no fear in love; but perfect love casts out fear....
We love Him because He first loved us.

1 JOHN 4:18-19 NKJV

Heaven on Earth

The High Places and the hinds' feet do not refer to heavenly places after death, but are meant to be the glorious experience of God's children here and now—if they will follow the path he chooses for them.

HANNAH HURNARD

I will bring the blind by a way they did not know;
I will lead them in paths they have not known.
I will make darkness light before them,
And crooked places straight.
These things I will do for them,
And not forsake them.

ISAIAH 42:16 NKJV

Our heavenly Father desires to give us more than heaven after earth. He has the power to give us heaven here on earth. As we listen to His heart, we find a purpose and a plan for our lives. Stepping out in faith to walk in God's will brings His heaven, His life force, His heart to our lives and to the lives of all we meet.

BARBARA FARMER

Have your heart right with Christ, and He will visit you often, and so turn weekdays into Sundays, meals into sacraments, homes into temples, and earth into heaven.

CHARLES H. SPURGEON

Peace for All Times

"Don't be afraid," said the Shepherd gently. *"You are in my service, and if you will trust me they will not be able to force you against your will."*

O LORD, no one but you can help the powerless against the mighty!
Help us, O LORD our God, for we trust in you alone.

2 CHRONICLES 14:11 NLT

The grace of God means something like: Here is your life. You might never have been, but you *are* because the party wouldn't have been complete without you. Here is the world. Beautiful and terrible things will happen. Don't be afraid. I am with you. Nothing can ever separate us. It's for you I created the universe. I love you.

FREDERICK BUECHNER

Fear not, for I am with you;
be not dismayed, for I am your God.
I will strengthen you, yes, I will help you,
I will uphold you with My righteous right hand.

ISAIAH 41:10 NKJV

The God of peace gives perfect peace
to those whose hearts are stayed upon Him.

CHARLES H. SPURGEON

Meeting the Shepherd

Much-Afraid remembered that the Chief Shepherd would then
be leading his flocks to their accustomed watering place beside a lovely
cascade and pool on the outskirts of the village. To this place she was
in the habit of going very early every morning to meet him and learn
his wishes and commands for the day, and again in the evenings
to give her report on the day's work. It was now time to meet him
there beside the pool, and she felt sure he would help her.

A quiet morning with a loving
God puts the events
of the upcoming day
into proper perspective.

JANETTE OKE

The LORD will command His lovingkindness in the daytime,
and in the night His song shall be with me—a prayer to the God of my life.

PSALM 42:8 NKJV

Let the day suffice, with all its joys and failings, its little triumphs
and defeats. I'd happily, if sleepily, welcome evening as a time of rest,
and let it slip away, losing nothing.

KATHLEEN NORRIS

Prayer is the key that opens up the day to shining possibilities;
and prayer in the evening secures hope and peace throughout the night.

Realm of Love

"*It would indeed be best for you to leave the Valley [of Humiliation] for the High Places, and I will very willingly take you there myself. The lower slopes of those mountains on the other side of the river are the borderland of my Father's Kingdom, the Realm of Love. No Fears of any kind are able to live there because 'perfect love casteth out fear and everything that torments.'*"

CHIEF SHEPHERD

Love comes while we rest against our Father's chest.
Joy comes when we catch the rhythms of His heart.
Peace comes when we live in harmony with those rhythms.

KEN GIRE

I am convinced that nothing can ever separate us from God's love.
Neither death nor life, neither angels nor demons,
neither our fears for today nor our worries about tomorrow—
not even the powers of hell can separate us from God's love.

ROMANS 8:38 NLT

When one has once fully entered the realm of love, the world—
no matter how imperfect—becomes rich and beautiful,
for it consists solely of opportunities for love.

SØREN KIERKEGAARD

*God has not given us a spirit of fear,
but of power and of love and of a sound mind.*

2 TIMOTHY 1:7 NKJV

Finding Confidence

Much-Afraid stared at him in amazement. "Go to the High Places," she exclaimed, "and live there? Oh, if only I could! For months past the longing has never left me. I think of it day and night, but it is not possible. I could never get there. I am too lame." She looked down at her malformed feet as she spoke, and her eyes again filled with tears and despair and self-pity. "These mountains are so steep and dangerous. I have been told that only the hinds and the deer can move on them safely."

The lame will leap like a deer,
and those who cannot speak will sing for joy!
Springs will gush forth in the wilderness,
and streams will water the wasteland.

ISAIAH 35:6 NLT

Grant us, in all our doubts and uncertainties, that Your spirit of wisdom may save us from all false choices, through Jesus Christ our Lord.

BOOK OF COMMON PRAYER

When the cares of my heart are many,
your consolations cheer my soul.

PSALM 94:19 ESV

If the Lord is with us, we have no cause of fear.
His eye is upon us, His arm over us, His ear open to our prayer.

JOHN NEWTON

The High Places

"It is quite true that the way up to the High Places is both difficult and dangerous," said the Shepherd. "It has to be, so that nothing which is an enemy of Love can make the ascent and invade the Kingdom. Nothing blemished or in any way imperfect is allowed there, and the inhabitants of the High Places do need 'hinds' feet.'"

CHIEF SHEPHERD

True living devotion presupposes the love of God, indeed, it is itself a true love of Him in the highest form. Divine love, enlightening our soul and making us pleasing to God, is called grace. Giving us power to do good, it is called charity. When it reaches the point of perfection where it makes us earnestly, frequently and readily do good, it is called devotion.

FRANCIS DE SALES

Not that I have already…arrived at my goal, but I press on to take hold of that for which Christ Jesus took hold of me.

PHILIPPIANS 3:12 NIV

A new path lies before us;
We're not sure where it leads;
But God goes on before us,
Providing all our needs.
This path, so new, so different
Exciting as we climb,
Will guide us in His perfect will
Until the end of time.

LINDA MAURICE

Chosen Vessel

"Much-Afraid, I could make yours like hinds' feet also, and set you upon the High Places. You could serve me then much more fully and be out of reach of all your enemies. I am delighted to hear that you have been longing to go there, for, as I said before, I have been waiting for you to make that suggestion. Then," he added, with another smile, "you would never have to meet Craven Fear again."

CHIEF SHEPHERD

When we allow God the privilege of shaping our lives, we discover new depths of purpose and meaning. What a joyful thought to realize you are a chosen vessel for God—perfectly suited for His use.

JONI EARECKSON TADA

We are not capable of perfection; we will make mistakes and hit many false notes before this life is through. But the Lord doesn't give up on us, and we don't have to achieve perfection before He can use us.

GIGI GRAHAM TCHIVIDJIAN

Therefore, as God's chosen people,
holy and dearly loved,
clothe yourselves with compassion,
kindness, humility, gentleness and patience.

COLOSSIANS 3:12 NIV

Healing to Our Brokenness

"It is true," said the Shepherd, "that you would have to be changed before you could live on the High Places, but if you are willing to go with me, I promise to help you develop hinds' feet. Up there on the mountains, as you get near the real High Places, the air is fresh and invigorating. It strengthens the whole body and there are streams with wonderful healing properties, so that those who bathe in them find all their blemishes and disfigurements washed away."

Look not upon me with contempt,
Though soiled and marred I be,
The King found me—an outcast thing—
And set his love on me.

HANNAH HURNARD

I am convinced that God has built into all of us an appreciation of beauty and has even allowed us to participate in the creation of beautiful things and places. It may be one way God brings healing to our brokenness, and a way that we can contribute toward bringing wholeness to our fallen world.

MARY JANE WORDEN

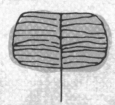

My child, pay attention to what I say.
Listen carefully to my words....
for they bring life to those who find them,
and healing to their whole body.

PROVERBS 4:20, 22 NLT

Transformed

*"Not only would I have to make your feet like hinds' feet,
but you would have to receive another name, for it would be as impossible
for a Much-Afraid to enter the Kingdom of Love as for any other member
of the Fearing family. Are you willing to be changed completely,
Much-Afraid, and to be made like the new name which you will receive
if you become a citizen in the Kingdom of Love?"*

CHIEF SHEPHERD

*Do not be conformed to this world, but be
transformed by the renewal of your mind, that by
testing you may discern what is the will of God,
what is good and acceptable and perfect.*

ROMANS 12:2 ESV

God is waiting...to transform us through every experience we have, waiting
for us to recognize Him in each move we make. We can make our lives
a prayer by becoming aware of God in each moment as we move through
our day, whether we're having a breathtaking moment of adventure
and beauty or performing a mundane task. God is the God of the present;
He is each moment and He wants to be found.

MIA POHLMAN

For [God] is, indeed, a wonderful Father who longs to pour
out His mercy upon us, and whose majesty is so great
that He can transform us from deep within.

TERESA OF ÁVILA

Love to Love

"*That is true,*" agreed the Shepherd. "*To love does mean to put yourself into the power of the loved one and to become very vulnerable to pain.... But it is so happy to love,*" said the Shepherd quietly. "*It is happy to love even if you are not loved in return. There is pain too, certainly, but Love does not think that very significant.*"

Love suffers long and is kind; love does not envy; love does not parade itself, is not puffed up; does not behave rudely, does not seek its own, is not provoked, thinks no evil; does not rejoice in iniquity, but rejoices in the truth; bears all things, believes all things, hopes all things, endures all things. Love never fails.

1 CORINTHIANS 13:4–8 NKJV

Out of pain and problems have come the sweetest songs, the most poignant poems, the most gripping stories. Out of suffering and tears have come the greatest spirits and the most blessed lives.

BILLY GRAHAM

Peace is not placidity: peace is
The power to endure the megatron of pain
With joy, the silent thunder of release,
The ordering of Love. Peace is the atom's start,
The primal image: God within the heart.

MADELEINE L'ENGLE

Pains of love be sweeter far
Than all other pleasures are.

JOHN DRYDEN

Guiding Love

"Thank you, thank you," she cried, and knelt at the Shepherd's feet. "How good you are. How patient you are. There is no one in the whole world as good and kind as you. I will go with you to the mountains. I will trust you to make my feet like hinds' feet, and to set me, even me, upon the High Places."

MUCH-AFRAID

*So faith bounds forward to its goal in God,
and love can trust her Lord to lead her there;
upheld by Him my soul is following hard,
till God hath full fulfilled my deepest prayer.*

FREDERICK BROOK

The LORD is my shepherd;
I shall not want.
He makes me to lie down in green pastures;
He leads me beside the still waters.
He restores my soul;
He leads me in the paths of righteousness
For His name's sake.

PSALM 23:1-3 NKJV

He Knows and Loves Us

The Chief Shepherd looked very kindly at the little shepherdess who had just received the seed of Love into her heart and was preparing to go with him to the High Places, but also with full understanding. He knew her through and through, in all the intricate labyrinth of her lonely heart, better far than she knew herself. No one understood better than he that growing into the likeness of a new name is a long process.

[God] knows everything about us. And He cares about everything.
Moreover, He can manage every situation. And He loves us!
Surely this is enough to open the wellsprings of joy....
And joy is always a source of strength.

HANNAH WHITALL SMITH

God possesses infinite knowledge and an awareness which is uniquely His.
At all times, even in the midst of any type of suffering, I can realize that He
knows, loves, watches, understands, and more than that, He has a purpose.

BILLY GRAHAM

God created the universe, but He also created you. God knows you,
God loves you, and God cares about the tiniest details of your life.

BRUCE BICKEL AND STAN JANTZ

Before I formed you in the womb I knew you,
before you were born I set you apart.

JEREMIAH 1:5 NIV

Of Very Tender Compassions

Much-Afraid was overwhelmed with shame that she had so quickly
acted like her old name and nature, which she had hoped was
beginning to be changed already. It seemed so impossible to ignore
the Fearings, still less to resist them. She did not dare look at the Shepherd,
but had she done so she would have seen with what compassion
he was regarding her. She did not realize that the Prince of Love
is "of very tender compassions to them that are afraid."

Praise the LORD, my soul,
and forget not all his benefits—
who forgives all your sins
and heals all your diseases,
who redeems your life from the pit
and crowns you with love and compassion,
who satisfies your desires with good things
so that your youth is renewed like the eagle's.

PSALM 103:2-5 NIV

We are so preciously loved by God
that we cannot even comprehend it.
No created being can ever know how much
and how sweetly and tenderly God loves them.

JULIAN OF NORWICH

The loving God we serve has immeasurable compassion
and tenderness toward each of us throughout our lives.

DR. JAMES DOBSON

Planted in Your Heart

*Suddenly she remembered, with a thrill of wonder and delight,
that the seed of Love had been planted in her heart. As she thought
of it, the same almost intolerable sweetness stole over her, the bittersweet,
indefinable but wholly delightful ecstasy of a new happiness.*

MUCH-AFRAID

*I pray that from his glorious, unlimited resources he will empower
you with inner strength through his Spirit. Then Christ will make
his home in your hearts as you trust in him. Your roots will
grow down into God's love and keep you strong.*

EPHESIANS 3:16-17 NLT

*Sooner or later we begin to understand that love is...here and now,
real and true, the most important thing in our lives. For love is the creator
of our favorite memories and the foundation of our fondest dreams.
Love is a promise that is always kept, a fortune that can never be spent,
a seed that can flourish in even the most unlikely of places.
And this radiance that never fades, this mysterious and magical joy,
is the greatest treasure of all—one known only by those who love.*

*Love is the seed of all hope.
It is the enticement to trust,
to risk, to try, to go on.*

GLORIA GAITHER

Hold On

*It came to her mind that he who understood her so well,
who knew all about her fears and had compassion on her,
would not leave until he was quite sure that she really meant to refuse
to go with him. Much-Afraid lifted her eyes, looked across the Valley
toward...the High Places.... Suddenly she remembered the last verse...*

*And then—in the dawn I saw him,
He whom my heart loveth so.
I found him, held him and told him
I never could let him go.*

*Let us hold unswervingly to the hope we profess,
for he who promised is faithful.*

HEBREWS 10:23 NIV

What is important is that you are holding on,
that you have got a grip on Christ and He will not let your hand go.

MOTHER TERESA

Grasp the fact that God is for you—let this certainty make its impact
on you in relation to what you are up against at this very moment;
and you will find in thus knowing God as your sovereign protector,
irrevocably committed to you in the covenant of grace,
both freedom from fear and new strength for the fight.

J. I. PACKER

God's hand is always there; once you grasp it you'll never want to let it go.

In the Garden

Sometimes the Shepherd and Much-Afraid walked over patches
of thousands of tiny little pink or mauve blossoms, each minutely small
and yet all together forming a brilliant carpet, far richer than
any seen in a king's palace.
Once the Shepherd stooped and touched the flowers gently with his fingers,
then said to Much-Afraid with a smile, "Humble yourself, and you will find
that Love is spreading a carpet of flowers beneath your feet."

There's not a tint that paints the rose
Or decks the lily fair,
Or marks the humblest flower that grows,
But God has placed it there.

So wait before the Lord. Wait in the stillness. And in that stillness,
assurance will come to you. You will know that you are heard;
you will know that your Lord ponders the voice of your humble desires;
you will hear quiet words spoken to you yourself,
perhaps to your grateful surprise and refreshment.

AMY CARMICHAEL

It is only a tiny rosebud—
A flower of God's design;
But I cannot unfold the petals
With these clumsy hands of mine.
For the pathway that lies before me
My Heavenly Father knows—
I'll trust Him to unfold the moments
Just as He unfolds the rose.

Nothing Wasted

*"I have often wondered about the wild flowers," Much-Afraid said.
"It does seem strange that such unnumbered multitudes should bloom
in the wild places of the earth where perhaps nobody ever sees them...
and the cattle can walk over them and crush them to death.
They have so much beauty and sweetness to give and no one on whom
to lavish it, nor who will even appreciate it."
The look the Shepherd turned on her was very beautiful.
"Nothing my Father and I have made is ever wasted," he said quietly.*

God does not waste our time. Every moment of our lives is precious
to Him, infinitely more precious than it is to us. Every experience
and person can lead us to God, and God is waiting to be found
in each moment of our day, waiting for us to allow the things
and people around us to cause us to remember Him.

MIA POHLMAN

We know that God causes all things to work together for good to those
who love God, to those who are called according to His purpose.

ROMANS 8:28 NASB

In the process of creation and relationship, what seems mundane
and trivial may show itself to be holy, precious, part of a pattern.

LUCI SHAW

*No love given away
is ever wasted!*

GLORIA GAITHER

Happy to Love

"The little wild flowers have a wonderful lesson to teach.
They offer themselves so sweetly and confidently and willingly,
even if it seems that there is no one to appreciate them.
Just as though they sang a joyous little song to themselves,
that it is so happy to love, even though one is not loved in return."

MUCH-AFRAID

*I have found a paradox that if I love until it hurts,
then there is no hurt, but only more love.*

MOTHER TERESA

Consider how the wild flowers grow. They do not labor or spin. Yet I tell
you, not even Solomon in all his splendor was dressed like one of these.
If that is how God clothes the grass of the field, which is here today, and
tomorrow is thrown into the fire, how much more will he clothe you.

LUKE 12:27-28 NIV

God's real love becomes more than a covering cloak.
It saturates our every cell.

ROSE GOBLE

There is more pleasure in loving than in being loved.

THOMAS FULLER

The Inner Soul

"I must tell you a great truth, Much-Afraid, which only the few understand. All the fairest beauties in the human soul, its greatest victories, and its most splendid achievements are always those which no one else knows anything about, or can only dimly guess at. Every inner response of the human heart to Love and every conquest over self-love is a new flower on the tree of Love."

CHIEF SHEPHERD

What seem our worst prayers may really be, in God's eyes, our best.... For these may come from a deeper level than feeling. God sometimes seems to speak to us most intimately when He catches us, as it were, off our guard.

C. S. LEWIS

Deep within us all there is an amazing inner sanctuary of the soul, a holy place...to which we may continuously return. Eternity is at our hearts, pressing upon our time-torn lives, warming us...calling us home unto Itself.

THOMAS R. KELLY

Within each of us there is an inner place where the living God Himself longs to dwell, our sacred center of belief.

Create in me a clean heart, O God,
And renew a steadfast spirit within me.

PSALM 51:10 NKJV

God waits for us in the inner sanctuary of the soul.
He welcomes us there.

RICHARD J. FOSTER

The Water Song

"The High Places are the starting places for the journey down to the lowest
place in the world. When you have hinds' feet and can go 'leaping on the
mountains and skipping on the hills,' you will be able, as I am, to run down
from the heights in gladdest self-giving and then go up to the mountains again.
You will be able to mount to the High Places swifter than eagles,
for it is only up on the High Places of Love that anyone can receive the power to
pour themselves down in an utter abandonment of self-giving."

CHIEF SHEPHERD

The Water Song
Come, oh come! let us away—
Lower, lower every day,
Oh, what joy it is to race
Down to find the lowest place.
This the dearest law we know—
"It is happy to go low."
Sweetest urge and sweetest will,
"Let us go down lower still."

HANNAH HURNARD

I live in a high and holy place, but also with the one who is contrite and lowly
in spirit, to revive the spirit of the lowly and to revive the heart of the contrite.

ISAIAH 57:15 NIV

Love's Own Language

"Only Love can really understand the music and the beauty and the joy
which was planted in the heart of all created things. Have you forgotten that
two days ago I planted the seed of Love in your heart? Already it has begun
to make you hear and see things which you did not notice before.
As Love grows in you, Much-Afraid, you will come to understand many
things which you never dreamed of before. You will develop the gift
of understanding many 'unknown tongues' and you will learn
to speak Love's own language too."

CHIEF SHEPHERD

When the heart of your heart opens, you can take deep pleasure in the
company of the people around you. When you are open to the beauty,
mystery, and grandeur of ordinary existence, you understand that it always
has been beautiful, mysterious, and grand, and always will be.

TIMOTHY MILLER

All happenings, great and small,
are parables whereby God speaks.
The art of life is to get the message.

MALCOLM MUGGERIDGE

I pray that your love will overflow more and more,
and that you will keep on growing in knowledge and understanding.

PHILIPPIANS 1:9 NLT

Give me a word, O Word of the Father: touch my heart;
enlighten the understandings of my heart.

LANCELOT ANDREWES

Becoming

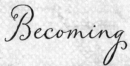

He looked at her most kindly, but answered quietly, "Much-Afraid, I could do what you wish. I could carry you all the way up to the High Places myself, instead of leaving you to climb there. But if I did, you would never be able to develop hinds' feet, and become my companion and go where I go. If you will climb to the heights this once with the companions I have chosen for you, even though it may seem a very long and in some places a very difficult journey, I promise you that you will develop hinds' feet."

CHIEF SHEPHERD

Affliction can be a means of refining and of purification. Many a life has come forth from the furnace of affliction more beautiful and more useful.

BILLY GRAHAM

These trials will show that your faith is genuine.
It is being tested as fire tests and purifies gold—
though your faith is far more precious than mere gold.

1 PETER 1:7 NLT

Character cannot be developed in ease and quiet.
Only through experience of trial and suffering can the soul be strengthened, vision cleared, ambition inspired, and success achieved.

HELEN KELLER

He knows the way that I take;
when he has tested me, I will come forth as gold.

JOB 23:10 NIV

Always There

"I assure you, however, that never for a moment shall I be beyond your reach or call for help, even when you cannot see me. It is just as though I shall be present with you all the time, even though invisible."

CHIEF SHEPHERD

When it's beyond our power and strength to make it on our own, we know beyond certainty that it was God, and not ourselves, that got us through. He receives greater glory when we are depleted, and cry out to Him for the strength to walk through the hardship.

REBECCA ST. JAMES

I know not where His islands lift

their fronded palms in air;

I only know I cannot drift

beyond His love and care.

JOHN GREENLEAF WHITTIER

God is our refuge and strength,
an ever-present help in trouble.
Therefore we will not fear, though the earth give way
and the mountains fall into the heart of the sea,
though its waters roar and foam
and the mountains quake with their surging.

PSALM 46:1-3 NIV

The Beauty of Trust

[Much-Afraid] turned to the Shepherd and said..., "I will trust you and do whatever you want."
Then, as she looked up in his face, he smiled most sweetly and said something he had never said before, "You have one real beauty, Much-Afraid, you have such trustful eyes. Trust is one of the most beautiful things in the world. When I look at the trust in your eyes I find you more beautiful to look upon than many a lovely queen."

Beauty is the mark God sets upon virtue.

RALPH WALDO EMERSON

A woman of beauty...knows in her quiet center where God dwells that He finds her beautiful, and deemed her worthy, and in Him, she is enough.

JOHN AND STASI ELDREDGE

The beauty of a woman must be seen from in her eyes, Because that is the doorway to her heart, the place where love resides.

SAM LEVENSON

This is how the holy women of old made themselves beautiful. They put their trust in God.

1 PETER 3:5 NLT

Nothing can compare to the beauty and greatness of the soul in which our King dwells in His full majesty.

TERESA OF ÁVILA

Following His Lead

"Do I wish to turn back? O Shepherd, to whom should I go? In all the world I have no one but you. Help me to follow you, even though it seems impossible. Help me to trust you as much as I long to love you."

MUCH-AFRAID

Faith means you want God and want to want nothing else.... In faith there is movement and development. Each day something is new.

BRENNAN MANNING

Whom have I in heaven but you?
And there is nothing on earth that I desire besides you.
My flesh and my heart may fail,
but God is the strength of my heart and my portion forever.

PSALM 73:25-26 ESV

God guides us, despite our uncertainties and our vagueness, even through our failings and mistakes.... He leads us step by step, from event to event. Only afterwards, as we look back over the way we have come...do we experience the feeling of having been led without knowing it, the feeling that God has mysteriously guided us.

PAUL TOURNIER

Faith never knows where it is being led,
but it loves and knows the One who is leading.

OSWALD CHAMBERS

My Deliverer

"Others have gone this way before me," she thought, "and they could even sing about it afterwards. Will he who is so strong and gentle be less faithful and gracious to me, weak and cowardly though I am, when it is so obvious that the thing he delights in most of all is to deliver his followers from all their fears and to take them to the High Places?"

MUCH-AFRAID

[God] stands fast as your rock, steadfast as your safeguard,
sleepless as your watcher, valiant as your champion.

CHARLES R. SPURGEON

I will love You, O LORD, my strength.
The LORD is my rock and my fortress and my deliverer;
My God, my strength, in whom I will trust;
My shield and the horn of my salvation, my stronghold.

PSALM 18:1-3 NKJV

*Do not take over much thought
for tomorrow. God,
who has led you safely on so far,
will lead you on to the end.*

FRANCIS DE SALES

[God] delights to meet the faith of one who looks up to Him and says,
"Lord, You know that I cannot do this—but I believe that You can!"

AMY CARMICHAEL

Secret Places

It would have been a curious sight, had there been anyone to watch, as Much-Afraid started on her journey, limping toward the High Places.... But there was no one there to see, for if there is one thing more certain than another, it is that the development of hinds' feet is a secret process, demanding that there should be no onlookers.

Retire from the world each day to some private spot.... Stay in the secret place till the surrounding noises begin to fade out of your heart and a sense of God's presence envelops you.... Listen for the inward Voice till you learn to recognize it.... Give yourself to God and then be what and who you are without regard to what others think.... Learn to pray inwardly every moment.

A. W. TOZER

God reads the secrets of the heart.
God reads its most intimate feelings,
even those which we are not aware of.

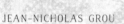

JEAN-NICHOLAS GROU

Contemplation is nothing else but a secret, peaceful, and loving infusion of God, which, if admitted, will set the soul on fire with the spirit of love.

JOHN OF THE CROSS

I will give you hidden treasures, riches stored in secret places,
so that you may know that I am the Lord,
the God of Israel, who summons you by name.

ISAIAH 45:3 NIV

Our Faithful God

The urge to turn back seemed almost irresistible, but at that moment when she stood, held in the clutch of Pride...she had an inner vision of the face of the Shepherd. She remembered the look with which he had promised her, *"I pledge myself to bring you there, and that you shall not be put to shame."*

Whatever mistakes we may make, we shall come safely home. Slippings and strayings there will be, no doubt, but the everlasting arms are beneath us; we shall be caught, rescued, restored. This is God's promise; this is how good He is. And our self-distrust, while keeping us humble, must not cloud the joy with which we lean on our faithful covenant God.

J. I. PACKER

God loves to look at us, and loves it when we will look back at Him. Even when we try to run away from our troubles...God will find us, bless us, even when we feel most alone, unsure.... God will find a way to let us know that He is with us in this place, wherever we are.

KATHLEEN NORRIS

He will cover you with his feathers,
and under his wings you will find refuge;
his faithfulness will be your shield and rampart.

PSALM 91:3-4 NIV

I know that God is faithful. I know that He answers prayers, many times in ways I may not understand.

SHEILA WALSH

For the Best to Become Possible

"Show us another way. Make a way for us, Shepherd, as you promised."
He looked at her and answered very gently, "That is the path,
Much-Afraid, and you are to go down there."
"Oh, no," she cried. "You can't mean it. You said if I would trust you,
you would bring me to the High Places, and that path leads right away
from them. It contradicts all that you promised."
"No," said the Shepherd, "it is not contradiction, only postponement
for the best to become possible."

*God wants to continually add to us, to develop
and enlarge us—always building on what
He has already taught and built in us.*

A. B. SIMPSON

In waiting we begin to get in touch with the rhythms of life—
stillness and action, listening and decision. They are the rhythms of God.
It is in the everyday and the commonplace that we learn patience,
acceptance, and contentment.

RICHARD J. FOSTER

 I will wait for the LORD.... I will put my trust in him.

ISAIAH 8:17 NIV

God, I have so many questions and so few answers. Reveal to me Your will.
Show me Your path and give me the wisdom to follow it....
When the questions of life are confusing or overwhelming,
remind me to wait on You, the One who has all the answers. Amen.

MARILYN JANSEN

He Walks with Me

Then they began the descent into the desert, and at the first step Much-Afraid felt a thrill of the sweetest joy and comfort surge through her, for she found that the Shepherd himself was going down with them. She would not have Sorrow and Suffering as her only companions, but he was there too.

Incredible as it may seem, God wants our companionship. He wants to have us close to Him. He wants to be a father to us, to shield us, to protect us, to counsel us, and to guide us in our way through life.

BILLY GRAHAM

God came to us because God wanted to join us on the road, to listen to our story, and to help us realize that we are not walking in circles but moving toward the house of peace and joy.

HENRI J. M. NOUWEN

Each of us may be sure that if God sends us on stony paths He will provide us with strong shoes, and He will not send us out on any journey for which He does not equip us well.

ALEXANDER MACLAREN

Even though I walk through the valley of the shadow of death, I fear no evil, for You are with me; Your rod and Your staff, they comfort me.

PSALM 23:4 NASB

Royalty

"Much-Afraid," he said, "all of my servants on their way to the High Places have had to make this detour through the desert.... Here they have learned many things which otherwise they would have known nothing about.... They came to learn the secret of royalty, and now you are here, Much-Afraid. You, too, are in the line of succession. It is a great privilege, and if you will, you also may learn the lesson of the furnace and of the great darkness.... Those who come down to the furnace go on their way afterwards as royal men and women."

CHIEF SHEPHERD

You are a chosen people, a royal priesthood, a holy nation, God's special possession, that you may declare the praises of him who called you out of darkness into his wonderful light.

1 PETER 2:9 NIV

You can come out of the furnace of trouble two ways: if you let it consume you, you come out a cinder; but there is a kind of metal which refuses to be consumed, and comes out a star.

JEAN CHURCH

All the way to heaven is heaven begun to [those who walk] near enough to God to hear the secrets He has to impart.

E. M. BOUNDS

He Is the Potter

They came to another and smaller room, in the center of which stood
a great wheel, flat, like a table. Beside it stood a potter who wrought
a work on the wheel. As he spun the wheel he fashioned his clay into many
beautiful shapes and objects. The material was cut and kneaded and shaped
as he saw fit, but always the clay lay still upon the wheel, submitting
to his every touch, perfectly, unresisting.
"Cannot I do with you, Much-Afraid, as this potter? Behold,
as the clay is in the hand of the potter so are you in my hand."

CHIEF SHEPHERD

*B*ack of all that seems to be, the Potter stands, with an ideal so lofty that
our highest imagination has not fully grasped it. A beauteous, transformed
life, fit to sit with Him upon His throne, is in the Potter's mind, and He is
shaping you through that which seemed a rude experience.

CHARLES HURLBURT AND T. C. HORTON

God gives shape to those things that do not
yet have any form. Just as Michelangelo "saw"
the sculpture inside the stone, so also God sees
what we cannot see. What is now hidden
from our sight will someday be revealed.

*N*ow, O Lord, you are our Father;
we are the clay, and you are our potter;
we are all the work of your hand.

ISAIAH 64:8 ESV

Acceptance with Joy

"What is your name, little flower...."
"Behold me! My name is Acceptance-with-Joy."...
Somehow the answer of the little golden flower which grew all alone in the
waste of the desert stole into her heart and echoed there faintly but sweetly,
filling her with comfort. She said to herself, "He has brought me here when
I did not want to come for his own purpose. I, too, will look up into his face
and say, 'Behold me! I am thy little handmaiden Acceptance-with-Joy'"

MUCH–AFRAID

When you accept the fact that sometimes seasons are dry and times
are hard and that God is in control of both, you will discover a sense
of divine refuge, because the hope then is in God and not in yourself.

CHARLES R. SWINDOLL

The desert and the parched land will be glad;
the wilderness will rejoice and blossom....
Then will the lame leap like a deer,
and the mute tongue shout for joy.
Water will gush forth in the wilderness
and streams in the desert.

ISAIAH 35:1, 6 NIV

Finding acceptance with joy, whatever the circumstances of life—
whether they are petty annoyances or fiery trials—this is a living faith that grows.

MARY LOU STEIGLEDER

Whenever You Call Me

"Remember, even though you seem to be farther away than ever from the High Places and from me, there is really no distance at all separating us. I can cross the desert sands as swiftly as I can leap from the High Places to the valleys, and whenever you call for me, I shall come. This is the word I now leave with you. Believe it and practice it with joy. My sheep hear my voice and they follow me."

CHIEF SHEPHERD

God is the shepherd in search of His lamb. His legs are scratched, His feet are sore, and His eyes are burning. He scales the cliffs and traverses the fields. He explores the caves. He cups His hands to His mouth and calls into the canyon. And the name He calls is yours.

MAX LUCADO

Oh come, let us worship and bow down,
Let us kneel before the LORD our Maker.
For He is our God,
And we are the people of His pasture,
And the sheep of His hand.

PSALM 95:6-7 NKJV

Abandon yourself to His care and guidance,
as a sheep in the care of a shepherd,
and trust Him utterly.

HANNAH WHITALL SMITH

Joy Springs Eternal

Though [Much-Afraid] went with Sorrow and Suffering day after day
along the shores of the great sea of Loneliness, she did not go cringingly
or complainingly. Indeed, gradually an impossible thing seemed
to be happening. A new kind of joy was springing up in her heart,
and she began to find herself noticing beauties in the landscape
of which until then she had been quite unconscious.

You are never alone. In your heart of hearts, in the place where
no two people are ever alike, Christ is waiting for you.
And what you never dared hope for springs to life.

ROGER OF TAIZÉ

If peace be in the heart, the wildest winter storm is full of solemn beauty.
The midnight flash but shows the path of duty,
Each living creature tells some new and joyous story,
The very trees and stones all catch a ray of glory,
If peace be in the heart.

C. F. RICHARDSON

I have known art and beauty, music and gladness; I have known friendship
and love and family ties; but it is certain that till we see God in the world—
God in the bright and boundless universe—we never know the highest joy.

ORVILLE DEWEY

O satisfy us in the morning with Your lovingkindness,
That we may sing for joy and be glad all our days.

PSALM 90:14 NASB

Deliver Me from Evil

Much-Afraid lifted her face toward the seemingly empty sky,
and with all her strength called out, "Come to my deliverance
and make no tarrying, O my Lord."
To the horror of the four ruffians, there was the Shepherd himself,
leaping toward them along the narrow promontory more terrible
than a great mountain stag with thrusting horns.

Beneath God's watchful eye
His saints securely dwell;
That Hand which bears all nature up
Shall guard His children well.

WILLIAM COWPER

If you say, "The LORD is my refuge,"
and you make the Most High your dwelling,
no harm will overtake you,
no disaster will come near your tent.
For he will command his angels concerning you
to guard you in all your ways;
they will lift you up in their hands,
so that you will not strike your foot against a stone.

PSALM 91:9-12 NIV

Do not look forward to the changes and chances
of this life in fear; rather look to them with full hope that, as they arise,
God, whose you are, will deliver you out of them.

FRANCIS DE SALES

Worth the Wait

Suddenly the path took another turn...not toward the mountains at all, but southward.... "Hope deferred maketh the heart sick," said the wise man of long ago, and how truly he spoke!...
"My Lord, what dost thou want to say to me? Speak—for thy servant heareth." Next moment the Shepherd was standing beside her. "Be of good cheer," he said, "it is I, be not afraid. Build me another altar and lay down your whole will as a burnt offering."...
Obediently Much-Afraid...laid down her will and said...
"I delight to do thy will, O my God."

We believers also groan, even though we have the Holy Spirit within us as a foretaste of future glory, for we long for our bodies to be released from sin and suffering. We, too, wait with eager hope for the day when God will give us our full rights as his adopted children, including the new bodies he has promised us.

ROMANS 8:23 NLT

The best we can hope for in this life is a knothole peek at the shining realities ahead. Yet a glimpse is enough. It's enough to convince our hearts that whatever sufferings and sorrows currently assail us aren't worthy of comparison to that which waits over the horizon.

JONI EARECKSON TADA

Be quiet, why this anxious heed
About thy tangled ways?
God knows them all, He giveth speed,
And He allows delays.

E. W.

Oasis in the Desert

Much-Afraid told herself that never before had she realized what the awakening from the death of winter was like. Perhaps it had needed the desert wastes to open her eyes to all this beauty.

When you accept the fact that sometimes seasons are dry and times are hard and that God is in control of both, you will discover a sense of divine refuge, because the hope then is in God and not in yourself.

CHARLES R. SWINDOLL

Behold, the winter is past;

the rain is over and gone.

The flowers appear on the earth,

the time of singing has come,

SONG OF SOLOMON 2:11-12 ESV

Into the wilderness of my lost way He comes to find me and lead me out. Into the desert of my barren life enters Jehovah and makes all the desert a garden.

CHARLES HURLBURT AND T. C. HORTON

After winter comes the summer. After night comes the dawn. And after every storm, there comes clear, open skies.

SAMUEL RUTHERFORD

Precious Tears

Much-Afraid's tears were all in secret, for no one but her enemies knew about this strange journey on which she had set out. The heart knoweth its own sorrow and there are times when, like David, it is comforting to think that our tears are put in a bottle and not one of them forgotten by the one who leads us in paths of sorrow.

You keep track of all my sorrows.
You have collected all my tears in your bottle.
You have recorded each one in your book.

PSALM 56:8 NLT

There is a sacredness in tears. They are not the mark of weakness, but of power. They speak more eloquently than 10,000 tongues. They are the messengers of overwhelming grief, of deep contrition and of unspeakable love.

WASHINGTON IRVING

Only God can heal the sorrow you feel. His gifts of peace, comfort, and compassion may feel elusive at times. But remember, feelings don't paint an accurate picture of the truth. Keep reaching out to Him, even when tears are all you have to offer.

The LORD is close to the brokenhearted
and saves those who are crushed in spirit.

PSALM 34:18 NIV

No Comparison

As the sun rose higher...she saw that the highest peaks were covered with snow, so white and glittering that her eyes were dazzled with their glory. She was looking at the High Places themselves.... Much-Afraid fell on her knees on the hilltop, bowed her head and worshiped. It seemed to her at that moment that all the pain and the postponement, all the sorrows and trials of the long journey she had made, were as nothing compared to the glory which shone before her.

Look toward heaven, look beyond the clouds, and you will see that the sufferings that you are undergoing here are nothing compared to the glory that God has prepared for you.

BILLY GRAHAM

If we are children, then we are heirs—heirs of God and co-heirs with Christ, if indeed we share in his sufferings in order that we may also share in his glory. I consider that our present sufferings are not worth comparing with the glory that will be revealed in us.

ROMANS 8:17–18 NIV

There are those who suffer greatly, and yet, through the recognition that pain can be a thread in the pattern of God's weaving, find the way to a fundamental joy.

If God hath made this world so fair,
Where sin and death abound,
How beautiful beyond compare
Will paradise be found!

JAMES MONTGOMERY

The Strength of His Presence

"Why, Much-Afraid." It was the Shepherd's voice close beside her. "What is
the matter? Be of good cheer, it is I, be not afraid."
He sounded so cheery and full of strength, and, moreover, without a hint
of reproach, that Much-Afraid felt as though a strong and exhilarating
cordial had been poured into her heart and that a stream of courage
and strength was flowing into her from his presence.

As sure as ever God puts
His children in the furnace
He will be in the furnace with them.

CHARLES H. SPURGEON

Even the youths shall faint and be weary,
And the young men shall utterly fall,
But those who wait on the LORD
Shall renew their strength;
They shall mount up with wings like eagles,
They shall run and not be weary,
They shall walk and not faint.

ISAIAH 40:30-31 NKJV

Look back from where we have come.
The path was at times an open road of joy,
At others a steep and bitter track of stones and pain.
How could we know the joy without the suffering?
And how could we endure the suffering but that we are
warmed and carried on the breast of God?

DESMOND M. TUTU

His Tender Compassion

The shame in her eyes met no answering reproach in his, and suddenly she found words echoing in her heart which other trembling souls had spoken. "My Lord is of very tender compassion to them that are afraid." As she looked, thankfulness welled up in her heart and the icy hand of fear which had clutched her broke and melted away and joy burst into bloom.

MUCH-AFRAID

When times get hard, remember Jesus. When people don't listen, remember Jesus. When tears come, remember Jesus. When disappointment is your bedpartner, remember Jesus. When fear pitches his tent in your front yard. When death looms, when anger singes, when shame weighs heavily. Remember Jesus.

MAX LUCADO

We sometimes fear to bring our troubles to God, because they must seem so small to Him who sits on the circle of the earth. But if they are large enough to [concern us] and endanger our welfare, they are large enough to touch His heart of love.

R. A. TORREY

The Lord's lovingkindnesses indeed never cease,
For His compassions never fail.
They are new every morning;
Great is Your faithfulness.

LAMENTATIONS 3:22-23 NASB

He Knows You

Much-Afraid trembled.... "I don't think—I want—hinds' feet, if it means I have to go on a path like that."... Instead of looking either disappointed or disapproving, [the Chief Shepherd] actually laughed again. "Oh, yes you do," he said cheerfully. "I know you better than you know yourself, Much-Afraid. You want it very much indeed, and I promise you these hinds' feet."

Your Savior knows your breaking point. The bruising and crushing and melting process is designed to reshape you, not ruin you. Your value is increasing the longer He lingers over you.

CHARLES R. SWINDOLL

God not only knows us, but He values us highly in spite of all He knows. "You are worth more than many sparrows."... You and I are the creatures He prizes above the rest of His creation. We are made in His image, and He sacrificed His Son that each one of us might be one with Him.

JOHN FISHER

*Look at the birds of the air,
that they do not sow, nor reap nor gather into barns,
and yet your heavenly Father feeds them.
Are you not worth much more than they?*

MATTHEW 6:26 NASB

When I Am Weak

"*I never dreamed you would do anything like this! Lead me to an impassable precipice.... It's too—it's too—*" *She fumbled for words, and then burst out laughing.* "*Why, it's too preposterously absurd! It's crazy! Whatever will you do next?*"
The Shepherd laughed too. "*I love doing preposterous things,*" *he replied.* "*Why, I don't know anything more exhilarating and delightful than turning weakness into strength, and fear into faith, and that which has been marred into perfection.*"

The tragedies that now blacken and darken the very air of heaven for us will sink into their places in a scheme so august, so magnificent, so joyful, that we shall laugh for wonder and delight.

ARTHUR CHRISTOPHER BACON

He said to me, "My grace is sufficient for you, for my power is made perfect in weakness." Therefore I will boast all the more gladly of my weaknesses, so that the power of Christ may rest upon me. For the sake of Christ, then, I am content with weaknesses, insults, hardships, persecutions, and calamities. For when I am weak, then I am strong.

2 CORINTHIANS 12:9-10 ESV

Give yourself fully to Jesus—
He will use you to accomplish great things
on the condition that you believe much more
in His love than in your weakness.

MOTHER TERESA

The Spirit of Grace

[The Chief Shepherd] brought out a little bottle of cordial which he gave to Much-Afraid, telling her to drink a little at once and to make use of it if ever she felt giddy or faint on the way up. The label on the bottle read, "Spirit of Grace and Comfort," and when Much-Afraid had taken a drop or two she felt so revived and strengthened that she was ready to begin the ascent without any feeling of faintness.

We know that [God] gives us every grace, every abundant grace;
and though we are so weak of ourselves, this grace is able
to carry us through every obstacle and difficulty.

ELIZABETH ANN SETON

*Grace...like the Lord, the giver,
never fails from age to age.*

JOHN NEWTON

If God wants you to do something, He'll make it possible
for you to do it, but the grace He provides comes only
with the task and cannot be stockpiled beforehand.
We are dependent on Him from hour to hour, and the greater our
awareness of this fact, the less likely we are to faint or fail in a crisis.

LOUIS CASSELS

The God of all grace, who called you to his eternal glory in Christ,
after you have suffered a little while, will himself restore you
and make you strong, firm and steadfast.

1 PETER 5:10 NIV

Satisfied Heart

"I have borne and have not fainted; I have not ceased to love,
and Love helped me push through the crack in the rock until I could look
right out onto my Love the sun himself.... He shines upon me and makes me
to rejoice, and has atoned to me for all that was taken from me and done
against me. There is no flower in all the world more blessed or more satisfied
than I, for I look up to him as a weaned child and say, 'Whom have
I in heaven but thee, and there is none upon earth that I desire but thee.'"

THE LITTLE FLOWER IN THE CREVICE

In comparison with this big world, the human heart
is only a small thing. Though the world is so large,
it is utterly unable to satisfy this tiny heart.
Our ever-growing soul and its capacities can be satisfied
only in the infinite God. As water is restless until
it reaches its level, so the soul has no peace until it rests in God.

SADHU SUNDAR SINGH

O God, I have tasted Your goodness,
and it has both satisfied me
and made me thirsty for more.

A. W. TOZER

Taste and see that the LORD is good;
blessed is the one who takes refuge in him.

PSALM 34:8 NIV

Safe in the Storm

"These are the Forests of Danger and Tribulation,
and often the pine trees grow so tall and so closely together
that the path may seem quite dark. Storms are very frequent up here
on these slopes, but keep pressing forward, for remember that nothing
can do you any real harm while you are following the path of my will."

CHIEF SHEPHERD

The LORD says, "I will rescue those who love me.
I will protect those who trust in my name.
When they call on me, I will answer;
I will be with them in trouble.
I will rescue and honor them."

PSALM 91:14-15 NLT

Only Christ Himself, who slept in the boat in the storm and then spoke calm
to the wind and waves, can stand beside us when we are in a panic and say
to us Peace. It will not be explainable. It transcends human understanding.
And there is nothing else like it in the whole wide world.

ELISABETH ELLIOT

How much greater is my peace
when I find it has come in the midst
of the storm and not because
He stilled its forces.

LEITA TWYEFFORT

Even in the Dark

"*I am going to lead you through danger and tribulation, Much-Afraid, but you need not be the least bit afraid, for I shall be with you. Even if I lead you through the Valley of the Shadow itself you need not fear, for my rod and my staff will comfort you.*"

CHIEF SHEPHERD

You shall not be afraid of the terror by night,
Nor of the arrow that flies by day,
Nor of the pestilence that walks in darkness,
Nor of the destruction that lays waste at noonday....
Because you have made the LORD, who is my refuge,
Even the Most High, your dwelling place, no evil shall befall you.

PSALM 91:5-7, 9-10 NKJV

For all of you who are in a dark place that seems like it will not go away, may God grant to you the treasures of darkness and riches in secret places. And may you know that He is the Lord.

ROBIN JONES GUNN

Everything has its wonders,

even darkness and silence,

and I learn, whatever state I may be in,

therein to be content.

HELEN KELLER

A Place for Joy

[Much-Afraid] seemed more alive than ever before to beauty
and delight in the world around her. It seemed as though her senses
had been quickened in some extraordinary way, enabling her to enjoy
every little detail of her life; so that although her companions actually
were Sorrow and Suffering, she often felt an almost inexplicable joy and
pleasure at the same time. This would happen when she looked at the bright,
crackling flames in the log fire, or listened to the sound of lashing rain
overhead emphasizing the safety and peace within the hut.

We may ask, "Why does God bring thunderclouds and disasters
when we want green pastures and still waters?" Bit by bit,
we find behind the clouds, the Father's feet; behind the lightning,
an abiding day that has no night; behind the thunder, a still small voice
that comforts with a comfort that is unspeakable.

OSWALD CHAMBERS

Lord, lift up the light of Your countenance upon us.
You have put gladness in my heart....
I will both lie down in peace, and sleep;
For You alone, O Lord, make me dwell in safety.

PSALM 4:6–8 NKJV

Sorrows come to stretch out
spaces in the heart for joy.

EDWIN MARKHAM

A Thrilling Leap

*[Much-Afraid] began to realize that, cowardly though she was, there was
something in her which responded with a surge of excitement to the tests
and difficulties of the way better than to easier and duller circumstances.
It was true that fear sent a dreadful shuddering thrill through her,
but nevertheless it was a thrill, and she found herself realizing
with astonishment that even the dizzy precipice had been more to her
liking than this dreary plodding on and on.*

There's no thrill in easy sailing when the skies are clear and blue,
there's no joy in merely doing things which any one can do.
But there is some satisfaction that is mighty sweet to take,
when you reach a destination that you thought you'd never make.

EDGAR GUEST

*There will always be the unknown.
There will always be the unprovable. But faith
confronts those frontiers with a thrilling leap.
Then life becomes vibrant with adventure!*

DR. ROBERT SCHULLER

Huge waves that would frighten an ordinary swimmer produce a
tremendous thrill for the surfer who has ridden them.

OSWALD CHAMBERS

*You thrill me, Lord, with all you have done for me!
I sing for joy because of what you have done.*

PSALM 92:4 NLT

The Remedy of a Song

*At last, one afternoon, when the only word which at all described her
progress is to say that she was slithering along the path,
all muddy and wet and bedraggled from constant slips,
she decided to sing.... There was perfect silence as she sang.
The loud, sneering voices of her enemies had died away altogether.*

Deliver me from my enemies, O God;
be my fortress against those who are attacking me....
They return at evening, snarling like dogs....
See what they spew from their mouths—
the words from their lips are sharp as swords....
But you laugh at them, LORD....
You are my strength, I watch for you;
You, God, are my fortress....
I will sing of your strength,
in the morning I will sing of your love;
for you are my fortress,
my refuge in times of trouble.

PSALM 59:1, 6–9, 16 NIV

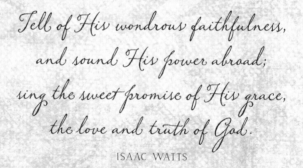

*Tell of His wondrous faithfulness,
and sound His power abroad;
sing the sweet promise of His grace,
the love and truth of God.*

ISAAC WATTS

Safe in His Hand

"*Shepherd! Help me!....*" Next instant she was clinging to him.... "O my Lord, don't let me leave you.... If you can deceive me, my Lord, about the promise and the hinds' feet and the new name or anything else, you may, indeed you may; only don't let me leave you. Don't let anything turn me back...." He lifted her up...and with his own hand wiped the tears from her cheeks, then said in his strong, cheery voice, "There is no question of your turning back, Much-Afraid. No one, not even your own shrinking heart, can pluck you out of my hand."

The reason we can dare to risk loving others is that "God has for Christ's sake loved us." Think of it! We are loved eternally, totally, individually, unreservedly! Nothing can take God's love away.

GLORIA GAITHER

My sheep hear My voice, and I know them, and they follow Me. And I give them eternal life, and they shall never perish; neither shall anyone snatch them out of My hand. My Father, who has given them to Me, is greater than all; and no one is able to snatch them out of My Father's hand.

JOHN 10:27–29 NKJV

The King of love my Shepherd is,
Whose goodness faileth never;
I nothing lack if I am His,
And He is mine forever.

SIR HENRY WILLIAMS BAKER

Walking with Him

"My sheep hear my voice, and they follow me. It is perfectly safe for you to go on in this way even though it looks so wrong, and now I give you another promise: Thine ears shall hear a word behind thee saying, 'This is the way, walk ye in it,' when ye turn to the right hand or to the left."

CHIEF SHEPHERD

So I went down into the garden,
The valley of buds and fruits,
To see if the pomegranates budded,
To look at the vinestock shoots.
And my soul in a burst of rapture,
Or ever I was aware,
Sped swifter than chariot horses,
For lo! he was waiting there.

HANNAH HURNARD

Although the Lord gives you the bread of adversity and the water of affliction, your teachers will be hidden no more; with your own eyes you will see them. Whether you turn to the right or to the left, your ears will hear a voice behind you, saying, "This is the way; walk in it."

ISAIAH 30:20-21 NIV

Joy is more than my spontaneous expression of laughter, gaiety, and lightness. It is deeper than an emotional expression of happiness. Joy is a growing, evolving manifestation of God in my life as I walk with Him.

BONNIE MONSON

Satisfaction

Other desires might clamor strongly and fiercely nearer the surface
of [Much-Afraid's] nature, but she knew now that down in the core
of her own being she was so shaped that nothing could fit,
fill, or satisfy her heart but he himself.

In the deepest heart of every man God planted
a longing for Himself, as He is: a God of love.

EUGENIA PRICE

As redemption creates the life of God in us, it also creates the things
which belong to that life. The only thing that can possibly satisfy
the need is what created the need. This is the meaning of redemption—
it creates and it satisfies.

OSWALD CHAMBERS

We are made for God, and nothing less will really satisfy us.

BRENNAN MANNING

My soul will be satisfied as with fat and rich food,
and my mouth will praise you with joyful lips.

PSALM 63:5 ESV

I thank You, O Lord, that You have so set eternity within my heart
that no earthly thing can ever wholly satisfy me.

JOHN BAILLIE

Content to Wait

It is true that when Much-Afraid looked at the mountains on the other side of the valley she wondered how they would ever manage to ascend them, but she found herself content to wait restfully and to wander in the valley as long as the Shepherd chose.

If our waiting begins by quieting the activities of daily life, and being still before God; if we bow and seek to see God in His universal and almighty operation; if we yield to Him in the assurance that He is working and will work in us; if we maintain the place of humility and stillness, and surrender until God's spirit has stirred up in us confidence that He will perfect His work, our waiting will indeed become the strength and the joy of the soul.

ANDREW MURRAY

When you're waiting, you're not doing nothing. You're doing the most important something there is. You're allowing your soul to grow up. If you can't be still and wait, you can't become what God created you to be.

SUE MONK KIDD

We walk without fear, full of hope and courage and strength to do His will, waiting for the endless good which He is always giving as fast as He can get us able to take it in.

GEORGE MACDONALD

In the morning, LORD, you hear my voice;
in the morning I lay my requests before you and wait expectantly.

PSALM 5:3 NIV

Becoming Beautiful

*One of the Shepherd's servants...had said, "Love is beautiful,
but it is also terrible—terrible in its determination to allow nothing blemished
or unworthy to remain in the beloved."
When she remembered this, Much-Afraid thought..."He will never be content
until he makes me what he is determined that I ought to be."*

The God who hears is also the one who speaks. He has spoken
and is still speaking. Humanity remains His project, not its own,
and His initiatives are always at work among us.

DALLAS WILLARD

*Purge me with hyssop, and I shall be clean;
wash me, and I shall be whiter than snow.
Let me hear joy and gladness;
let the bones that you have broken rejoice.*

PSALM 51:7-8 ESV

One of the greatest strains in life is the strain of waiting for God.
God takes us like a bow which He stretches, and at a certain point we say,
"I can't stand any more." But God does not heed. God goes on stretching
because He is aiming at His mark, not ours, and the patience needed
is that we hang in there until God lets the arrow fly.

OSWALD CHAMBERS

God's fingers can touch nothing but to mold it into loveliness.

GEORGE MACDONALD

Humble Hearts

"Does the joy of the waters seem to end when they break on the rock below?... At first sight perhaps the leap does look terrible," said the Shepherd, "but as you can see, the water itself finds no terror in it, no moment of hesitation or shrinking, only joy unspeakable, and full of glory, because it is the movement natural to it. Self-giving is its life.... You can see that as it obeys that glorious urge the obstacles which look so terrifying are perfectly harmless, and indeed only add to the joy and glory of the movement."

The way of ascending is humility; the way of descending is pride. If our heart is humble we shall be lifted to heaven.

BENEDICT OF NURSIA

As we enter more and more deeply into this experience of being humbled and exalted, our knowledge of God increases, and with it our peace, our strength, and our joy.

J. I. PACKER

Emptiness and fullness at first seem complete opposites. But in the spiritual life they are not. In the spiritual life we find the fulfillment of our deepest desires by becoming empty for God. We must empty the cups of our lives completely to be able to receive the fullness of life from God.

HENRI J. M. NOUWEN

God blesses those who are humble, for they will inherit the whole earth.

MATTHEW 5:5 NLT

Glimpse of Heaven

Every now and again, however, there would be a rent in the veil of mist, and then, as though framed in an open window, would appear a dazzling whiteness. For a moment one of the vanished peaks would gleam through the opening as if to say, "Be of good courage, we are all here, even though you cannot see us." Then the mist would swirl together again and the window in heaven would close.

Open my eyes that I may see
Glimpses of truth Thou hast for me.
Place in my hands the wonderful key
That shall unclasp and set me free:
Silently now I wait for Thee,
Ready, my God, Thy will to see;
Open my eyes, illumine me, Spirit divine!

CLARA H. SCOTT

In keeping with his promise we are looking forward to a new heaven
and a new earth, where righteousness dwells.

2 PETER 3:13 NIV

Lord, give me an open heart to find You everywhere, to glimpse the heaven
enfolded in a bud, and to experience eternity in the smallest act of love.

MOTHER TERESA

King of Love

*The Shepherd...was transfigured before her, and she knew him then
to be what she had dimly sensed all along—the King of Love himself....
He was clothed in a white garment glistening in its purity, but over it
he wore a robe of purple.... On his head he wore the crown royal, but...
the face that looked down upon her was that of the Shepherd whom
she had loved and followed.... His eyes were still full of gentleness
and tenderness but also of strength and power and authority.*

*He was transfigured before them,
and his face shone like the sun,
and his clothes became white as light.*

MATTHEW 17:2 ESV

*The more we know about Him the more wonderful He becomes,
and the more intimately we know Him the more precious He is....
He holds the world in the hollow of His hand as a dry leaf
and could crush it. But He so loved you and me that He laid aside
His royal robe, arrayed Himself in human flesh,
and then poured out His precious blood for us.*

CHARLES HURLBURT AND T. C. HORTON

*Realize the tremendous honor of serving the King of kings!
Serve Him worthily, not as an unwilling slave,
but as one chosen by love.*

BASILEA SCHLINK

Safe Shelter

*Side by side, they sat huddled together [in the cave shelter],
then all of a sudden the storm burst over them in frightful fury....
Then the rains descended and the floods came, and the winds blew and beat
upon the mountains until everything around them seemed to be shivering
and quaking and falling. Flood waters rushed down the steep cliffs
and a torrent poured over the rocks which projected over the cave so that
the whole entrance was closed with a waterfall, but not a single drop fell
inside the cave where the three sat together on the ground.*

*Perhaps He sees that the best waters for you to walk beside will be raging
waves of trouble and sorrow. If this should be the case, He will make
them still waters for you, and you must go and lie down beside them,
and let them have all their blessed influences upon you.*

HANNAH WHITALL SMITH

The Lord's our Rock, in Him we hide
Secure whatever ill betide...
The raging storms may round us beat
We'll never leave our safe retreat
O Rock divine, O Refuge dear,
Be Thou our Helper ever near
A Shelter in the time of storm.

VERNON J. CHARLESWORTH

*The rain descended, the floods came,
and the winds blew and beat on that house;
and it did not fall, for it was founded on the rock.*

MATTHEW 7:25 NKJV

No Matter What

*Into Much-Afraid's mind came the words which Bitterness
had flung at her...: "Sooner or later...he will put you on some sort
of a cross and abandon you to it."
It seemed that in a way Bitterness had been right...only he had been too
ignorant to know and she too foolish at that time to understand that in all the
world only one thing really mattered, to do the will of the one she followed
and loved, no matter what it involved or cost.*

The God of the universe is not something we can just add to our lives and
keep on as we did before. The Spirit who raised Christ from the dead is not
someone we can just call on when we want a little extra power in our lives.
Jesus Christ did not die in order to follow us, He died and rose again so that
we could forget everything else and follow Him to the cross, to true Life.

FRANCIS CHAN

Then Jesus said to his disciples, "Whoever wants to be my disciple must
deny themselves and take up their cross and follow me. For whoever wants
to save their life will lose it, but whoever loses their life for me will find it."

MATTHEW 16:24-25 NIV

*God did not tell us to follow Him
because He needed our help,
but because He knew that loving Him
would make us whole.*

IRENAEUS

My One Desire

Much-Afraid felt nothing but a great stillness in which only one desire remained, to do that which he had told her, simply because he had asked it of her. The cold, dull desolation which had filled her heart in the cave was gone completely; one flame burned there steadily, the flame of concentrated desire to do his will. Everything else had died down and fallen into ashes.

God led Jesus to a cross, not a crown, and yet that cross ultimately proved to be the gateway to freedom and forgiveness for every sinner in the world. God also asks us as Jesus' followers to carry a cross. Paradoxically, in carrying that cross, we find liberty and joy and fulfillment.

BILL HYBELS

God has promised us even more than His own Son.
He's promised us power through the Spirit—
power that will help us do all that He asks of us.

JONI EARECKSON TADA

We desire many things, and He offers us only one thing.
He *can* offer us only one thing—Himself.
He has nothing else to give. There *is* nothing else to give.

PETER KREEFT

I take joy in doing your will, my God,
for your instructions are written on my heart.

PSALM 40:8 NLT

Healing Waters

Much-Afraid remembered the healing streams of which
the Shepherd had spoken.... Stepping straight back into the pool
with a shock of sweetest pleasure and putting her head beneath the clear
waters, she splashed them about her face. Then she found a little pool
among the rocks, still and clear as a mirror. Kneeling down, she looked into
its unruffled surface and saw her face quite clearly. It was true, the ugly,
twisted mouth had vanished and the face she saw reflected back by
the water was as relaxed and perfect as the face of a little child.

*The Lamb at the center of the throne
will be their shepherd;
"he will lead them to springs of living water."
"And God will wipe away every tear from their eyes."*

REVELATION 7:17 NIV

From God, great and small, rich and poor, draw living water
from a living spring, and those who serve Him freely
and gladly will receive grace answering to grace.

THOMAS À KEMPIS

A pure spirit is a sparkling stream, full of clear thought,
and continually renewed in the crystal river of God's love.

JANET L. SMITH

God brings us into deep waters, not to drown us, but to cleanse us.

JOHN H. AUGHEY

Irresistible Beauty

Then it came again—tingling through her—a call ringing down from some high place above.... Every nerve in her body surged with desire to respond to the call, and Much-Afraid felt her feet and legs tingling with an almost irresistible urge to go bounding up the mountains.

We are of such value to God that He came to live among us...
and to guide us home. He will go to any length to seek us,
even to being lifted high upon the cross to draw us back to Himself.
We can only respond by loving God for His love.

CATHERINE OF SIENA

God who is goodness and truth is also beauty. It is this innate human
and divine longing, found in the company of goodness and truth,
that is able to recognize and leap up at beauty and rejoice
and know that all is beautiful, that there is not one speck of beauty
under the sun that does not mirror back the beauty of God.

ROBERTA BONDI

God's holy beauty comes near you, like a spiritual scent, and it stirs your drowsing soul.... He creates in you the desire to find Him and run after Him— to follow wherever He leads you.

JOHN OF THE CROSS

How lovely is your dwelling place, O LORD....
I long...to enter the courts of the LORD.

PSALM 84:1-2 NLT

Mountain Top

In a moment or two…Much-Afraid was leaping up the mountainside toward the peak above, from which the summons had come… He was there—standing on the peak—just as she had known he would be, strong and grand and glorious in the beauty of the sunrise, holding out both hands and calling to her with a great laugh, "You—with the hinds' feet—jump over here." She gave one last flying spring, caught his hands and landed beside him on the topmost peak of the mountain.

There is the firm commitment to the triumph of the human spirit over adversity, the certainty that there's a God on high who may not move mountains but will give you the strength to climb.

GENEVA SMITHERMAN

Why should we live halfway up the hill and swathed in the mists, when we might have an unclouded sky and a radiant sun over our heads if we would climb higher and walk in the light of His face?

ALEXANDER MACLAREN

Go on up to a high mountain…
lift up your voice with strength…
lift it up, fear not;
say to the cities of Judah,
"Behold your God!"

ISAIAH 40:9 ESV

My New Name

"At last you are here and the 'night of weeping is over and joy comes to you in the morning.'" Then, lifting her up, [the Chief Shepherd] continued, "This is the time when you are to receive the fulfillment of the promises. Never am I to call you Much-Afraid again.... This is your new name," he declared. "From henceforth you are Grace and Glory."

To the one who is victorious, I will give...that person a white stone with a new name written on it, known only to the one who receives it.

REVELATION 2:17 NIV

I could provide a long list of all...the hurts and missteps and conflicts.... But then come the golden moments and these are the times when [everyone] must stop and smile and clear the air.... It is here, in the uncluttered heart that the Author and Finisher of our faith writes new songs, new stories, new promises.

ROBIN JONES GUNN

The LORD God is a sun and shield; the LORD will give grace and glory; no good thing will He withhold from those who walk uprightly.

PSALM 84:11 NKJV

Today I only know my given name that may or may not suit me, but I know there will be a day when I am given a name that will completely reveal who I am in my Father's eyes.

BARBARA FARMER

When the Heart Blooms

*She laid bare her heart, and out came the sweetest perfume she
had ever breathed and filled all the air around them with its fragrance.
There in her heart was a plant whose shape and form could not
be seen because it was covered all over with pure white,
almost transparent blooms, from which the fragrance poured forth.*

*God has caused me to be fruitful
in the land of my affliction.*

GENESIS 41:52 NKJV

*I*f you will but believe your Father's Word, under that beating rain
are springing up spiritual flowers of such fragrance and beauty
as never before grew in that stormless, unchastened life of yours.
You indeed see the rain. But do you see also the flowers?
You are pained by the testings. But God sees the sweet flower
of faith which is upspringing in your life under those very trials.
You shrink from the suffering. But God sees the tender compassion
for other sufferers which is finding birth in your soul....
It isn't raining afflictions for you. It is raining tenderness, love, compassion,
patience, and a thousand other flowers and fruits of the blessed Spirit, which
are bringing into your life such a spiritual enrichment as all the fullness of
worldly prosperity and ease was never able to beget in your innermost soul.

J. M. MCC.

*A*s a rose fills a room with its fragrance, so will God's love fill our lives.

MARGARET BROWNLEY

Jewels for Your Crown

The Chief Shepherd said, "Give me the bag of stones of remembrance that you have gathered on your journey, Grace and Glory."
She took it out and passed it to him and then he bade her hold out her hands. On doing so, he opened the little purse and emptied the contents into her hands. Then she gasped again with bewilderment and delight, for instead of the common, ugly stones she had gathered from the altars along the way, there fell into her hands a heap of glorious, sparkling jewels, very precious and very beautiful. As she stood there, half-dazzled by the glory of the flashing gems, she saw in his hand a circlet of pure gold.

You shall be called by a new name,
Which the mouth of the LORD will name.
You shall also be a crown of glory
In the hand of the LORD,
And a royal diadem
In the hand of your God.

ISAIAH 62:2–3 NKJV

There is in store for me the crown of righteousness, which the Lord, the righteous Judge, will award to me on that day.

2 TIMOTHY 4:8 NIV

Blessed is the one who perseveres under trial because, having stood the test, that person will receive the crown of life that the Lord has promised to those who love him.

JAMES 1:12 NIV

Changed to Glory

*Supposing she had thrown them away, had discarded her trust
in his promises, had gone back on her surrenders to his will?
There could have been no jewels now to his praise and glory,
and no crown for her to wear.
She marveled at the grace and love and tenderness and patience which had
led and trained and guarded and kept poor faltering Much-Afraid, which had
not allowed her to turn back, and which now changed all her trials into glory.*

*Beloved, do not think it strange concerning the fiery trial which
is to try you, as though some strange thing happened to you;
but rejoice to the extent that you partake of Christ's sufferings,
that when His glory is revealed, you may also be glad with exceeding joy.*

1 PETER 4:12-13 NKJV

*Above all, know that God delights in you every second of the day
and night. No one is beyond His reach. The extent He's willing to go
to be in a relationship with you leads to the foot of the cross where He
reveals His deepest longing to join His heart to yours at any cost.*

MARSHA CROCKETT

*Like any other gift, the gift of grace
can be yours only if you'll reach out and take it.
Maybe being able to reach out
and take it is a gift too.*

FREDERICK BUECHNER

New Discoveries

Grace and Glory with her handmaidens Joy and Peace stayed up on the High Places for several weeks while all three explored the heights and learned many new lessons from the King. He led them himself to many places, and explained to them as much as they were able to understand at that time. He also encouraged them to explore on their own, for there are always new and lovely discoveries to make up there on the High Places.

As we grow in our capacities to see and enjoy the joys
that God has placed in our lives, life becomes a glorious
experience of discovering His endless wonders.

WENDY MOORE

With God, life is eternal—both in quality and length. There is no joy
comparable to the joy of discovering something new from God, about God.
If the continuing life is a life of joy, we will go on discovering, learning.

EUGENIA PRICE

One of the most wonderful things about knowing God is that there's
always so much more to know, so much more to discover.
Just when we least expect it, He intrudes into our neat
and tidy notions about who He is and how He works.

JONI EARECKSON TADA

*Come, let us go up to the mountain
of the LORD...that he may teach us his ways
and that we may walk in his paths.*

ISAIAH 2:3 ESV

Breathtaking View

*Grace and Glory never tired of looking from the glorious new viewpoint
on the first slopes of the Kingdom of Love and seeing it all from
a new perspective. What she could see and could take in almost
intoxicated her with joy and thanksgiving, and sometimes even
with inexpressible relief. Things which she had thought dark and terrible
and which had made her tremble as she looked up from the Valley
because they had seemed so alien to any part of the Realm of Love
were now seen to be but parts of a great and wonderful whole.*

Live your life each day as you would climb a mountain. An occasional
glance toward the summit keeps the goal in mind, but many beautiful
scenes are to be observed from each new vantage point. Climb slowly,
steadily, enjoying each passing moment; and the view from the summit
will serve as a fitting climax for the journey.

HAROLD V. MELCHERT

*Now we see in a mirror dimly, but then face
to face; now I know in part, but then I will know
fully just as I also have been fully known.*

1 CORINTHIANS 13:12 NASB

My life is but a weaving between my Lord and me,
I cannot choose the colors He worketh steadily.
Oftimes He weaveth sorrow, and I in foolish pride
Forget He sees the upper and I, the underside.
The dark threads are as needful in the Weaver's skillful hand
As the threads of gold and silver in the pattern He has planned.

A Queen Already

"I learned...that you, my Lord, never regarded me as I actually was,
lame and weak and crooked and cowardly. You saw me as I would
be when you had done what you promised and had brought me
to the High Places, when it could be truly said, 'There is none that walks
with such a queenly ease, nor with such grace, as she.' You always
treated me with the same love and graciousness as though I were a queen
already and not wretched little Much-Afraid."

GRACE AND GLORY

The God of the universe—the One who created everything and holds
it all in His hands—created each of us in His image, to bear His likeness,
His imprint. It is only when Christ dwells within our hearts, radiating the pure
light of His love through our humanity, that we discover who we are
and what we were intended to be.

WENDY MOORE

Imagine yourself as a living house. God comes in to rebuild that house....
You thought you were going to be made into a decent little cottage:
but He is building a palace. He intends to come and live in it Himself.

C. S. LEWIS

Therefore, if anyone is in Christ,
he is a new creation.
The old has passed away;
behold, the new has come.

2 CORINTHIANS 5:17 ESV

Overcoming

"*Every circumstance in life, no matter how crooked and distorted and ugly it appears to be, if it is reacted to in love and forgiveness and obedient to your will can be transformed. Therefore...you purposely allow us to be brought into contact with the bad and evil things that you want changed. Perhaps that is the very reason that we are here in this world...so that we may let you teach us so to react to them, that out of them we can create lovely qualities to live forever.... Not simply binding [evil] so that it cannot work harm, but whenever possible overcoming it with good.*"

GRACE AND GLORY

The cross is a way of life; the way of love meeting all hate with love, all evil with good, all negatives with positives.

RUFUS MOSELEY

You, dear children, are from God and have overcome them, because the one who is in you is greater than the one who is in the world.

1 JOHN 4:4 NIV

I can do all things through Christ who strengthens me.

PHILIPPIANS 4:13 NKJV

*I*t was with people like ourselves that Jesus set out to change the world—and did it.

CAROLYN LYNN

Dare to Love the World

"So remember this; as long as you are willing to be Acceptance-with-Joy and Bearing-in-Love, you can never again be crippled, and you will be able to go wherever I lead you. You will be able to go down into the Valley of the world to work with me there, for that is where the evil and sorrowful and ugly things are which need to be overcome."

CHIEF SHEPHERD

Love makes burdens lighter, because you divide them. It makes joys more intense, because you share them. It makes you stronger, so that you can reach out and become involved with life in ways you dared not risk alone.

Let us have faith that right makes might, and in that faith let us to the end dare to do our duty as we understand it.

ABRAHAM LINCOLN

In His mercy God has chosen us, unworthy as we are, out of this world to serve Him and thus to advance in goodness and to bear the greatest possible purity of love in patience.

ANTHONY ZACHARY

Be strong in the Lord and in the strength of his might. Put on the whole armor of God, that you may be able to stand.

EPHESIANS 6:10–11 ESV

Turnabout

As Grace and Glory sat looking down into the [Valley of Humiliation]... she discovered that her feelings toward her relatives and those who lived down there...had undergone a complete change, and she saw them in a new light. She had thought of them only as horrible enemies, but now she realized that they were just miserable beings such as she had been herself. They were indwelt and tormented...just as she had been by her fears. They were wretched slaves to the natures which gave them their names, and the more horrible the qualities which characterized them, the more misery they endured, and the more we should show them compassion.

Christ has no body on earth but yours, no hands but yours, no feet but yours. Yours are the eyes through which Christ's compassion for the world is to look out; yours are the feet with which He is to go about doing good; and yours are the hands with which He is to bless us now.

TERESA OF ÁVILA

True love possesses the ability to see beyond.... It goes beyond mere words. It sees beneath the veneer. Love focuses on the soul. Love sees another's soul in great need of help and sets compassion to work.

CHARLES R. SWINDOLL

How are they to believe in him of whom they have never heard?... As it is written, "How beautiful are the feet of those who preach the good news!"

ROMANS 10:14–15 ESV

Ambassadors

Then Peace (who before had been [called] Suffering) said quietly, "I have noticed that when people are brought into sorrow and suffering, or loss, or humiliation, or grief, or into some place of great need, they sometimes become ready to know the Shepherd and to seek his help."
"Yes!" exclaimed Grace and Glory, "I am sure you are right. Oh, if only we could go to them! If only there were some way of helping them to find what we have found."

Jesus...not only has a great compassion in His heart, but...He has a special and a particular compassion measured out according to every individual man's measure of need, according to every individual man's specialty, and particularity and singularity, and secrecy of need.

THOMAS GOODWIN

It doesn't take a huge spotlight to draw attention to how great our God is. All it takes is for one committed person to so let his light shine before men, that a world lost in darkness welcomes the light.

GARY SMALLEY AND JOHN TRENT

Our Father is preparing us to meet the deep inner needs of others by bringing us through the dark places first.

CHARLES R. SWINDOLL

Praise be to...the God of all comfort, who comforts us in all our troubles, so that we can comfort those in any trouble with the comfort we ourselves receive from God.

2 CORINTHIANS 1:3-4 NIV

Light of the World

Suddenly Grace and Glory understood. She was beholding a wondrous and glorious truth: "A great multitude whom no man could number" brought like herself by the King to the Kingdom of Love and to the High Places so that they could now pour out their lives in gladdest abandonment, leaping down with him to the sorrowful, desolate places below, to share with others the life which they had received....
She, too, at last, was to go down with them, pouring herself forth in Love's abandonment of Self-giving. "He brought me to the heights just for this," she whispered to herself.

To build in darkness does require faith. But one day the light returns and you discover that you have become a fortress which is impregnable to certain kinds of trouble; you may even find yourself needed and sought by others as a beacon in their dark.

OLGA ROSMANITH

Everybody can be great...because anybody can serve.
You don't have to have a college degree to serve....
You only need a heart full of grace. A soul generated by love.

MARTIN LUTHER KING JR.

You are the light of the world.
A city set on a hill cannot be hidden.

MATTHEW 5:14 NASB

Begin today! No matter how feeble the light, let it shine as best it may. The world may need just that quality of light which you have.

HENRY C. BLINN

Ellie Claire® Gift & Paper Expressions
Franklin, TN 37067
EllieClaire.com
Ellie Claire is a registered trademark of Worthy Media, Inc.

Hinds' Feet on High Places Journal
© 2015 by Ellie Claire
Published by Ellie Claire, an imprint of Worthy Publishing Group,
a division of Worthy Media, Inc.

ISBN 978-1-63326-055-9

Stock or custom editions of Ellie Claire titles may be purchased in bulk for educational,
business, ministry, fundraising, or sales promotional use. For information, please
e-mail info@EllieClaire.com

Compiled by Barbara Farmer

Printed in China

1 2 3 4 5 6 7 8 9 – 20 19 18 17 16 15